Did You Know That...?

Becca Heddle

OXFORD
UNIVERSITY PRESS

OXFORD
UNIVERSITY PRESS

is a department of the University of Oxford.
It furthers the University's objective of excellence in research, scholarship,
and education by publishing worldwide in

Oxford New York
Auckland Cape Town Dar es Salaam Hong Kong Karachi
Kuala Lumpur Madrid Melbourne Mexico City Nairobi
New Delhi Shanghai Taipei Toronto

With offices in

Argentina Austria Brazil Chile Czech Republic France Greece
Guatemala Hungary Italy Japan Poland Portugal Singapore
South Korea Switzerland Thailand Turkey Ukraine Vietnam

First published 2007

British Library Cataloguing in Publication Data

Data available

ISBN: 978-0-19-846130-2

5 7 9 10 8 6

Printed in China by Imago

Paper used in the production of this book is a natural,
recyclable product made from wood grown in sustainable forests.
The manufacturing process conforms to the environmental
regulations of the country of origin.

Acknowledgements

The publisher would like to thank the following for permission to reproduce photographs: **p4**t Alamy/Chuck Pefley, **p4**l Alamy/Ace Stock Ltd, **p4**c Alamy/Steven May, **p5**l Corbis/Ashley Cooper, **p5**r Corbis/A Inden/Zefa, **p6**r Alamy/Kevin Schafer, **p6**l Corbis/Tim Davies, **p7** Frank Lane Picture Agency/Mitsuaki Iwago/Minden Pictures, **p8** Corbis/Kevin Schafer, **p9** Alamy/Dave Watts, **p10** Corbis/David Muench, **p11** Dorling Kindersley, **p11**b Alamy/Philip Bramhill, **p12** Alamy/Reinhard Dirscherl, **p13** Corbis/Jeffrey L Rotman, **p14**tl Ancient Art & Architecture, **p14**c Alamy/Robert Estall, **p14**c Alamy/Dominic Burke, **p14**b Getty Images/Tim Graham Photo Library, **p15** Corbis/Wu Hong/epa, **p16** Mark Anderson, **p16**b FLPA/Mark Newman, **p17** Alamy/Chuck Pefley, **p18** Alamy/Robert Harding Picture Library, **p19**t Corbis/Wolfgang Kaehler, **p19**b Alamy/Mark Hamilton, **p20**l Alamy/AM Corporation, **p21**t Alamy/Andrew Bargery, **p21**b Corbis/Svenja-foto/Zefa, **p22** Corbis/Werner H Mueller, **p23**t Corbis, **p23**b Brian Tarr Photography/Photographers Direct

Cover: OUP/Classet

Illustrations by Martin Aston: **p7**, **p9**, Julian Baker: **p18**, Barking Dog Art: **p22**, Martin Cottam: **p20**, Roger Gorringe: **p8**, **p12**, **p13**

Designed by Bigtop

Contents

We think we know . . .

We all think we know how the world works. Here are some of the things we think we know.

Birds fly.

Female, not male, animals bear young.

Birds lay eggs – animals don't.

Things fall down when you throw them up.

Water makes things wet.

What if these things aren't always true? That might make the world a confusing place. Or it might make it even more interesting than you thought it was!

This book is all about things that don't work the way we expect them to. Some of them are to do with nature, and some are to do with the things that people make, breaking rules that we have invented ourselves.

Wings and things

What is a bird? We think it's an animal which has wings, lays eggs and flies, but some birds don't fly at all!

Look at this bird from New Zealand – a kiwi. Its wings are too small to see, and they are no use at all.

The kiwi is not even shaped much like a bird.

Penguins don't look much like birds either. Their wings are used more like flippers, and they only 'fly' under water when they swim.

Emus and ostriches are huge birds with long legs. They run very fast instead of flying. They are also good swimmers.

Ostriches are the fastest birds in the world.

Flightless birds are most likely to come from places where there are no animals to eat them – they don't need to fly to escape.

Dodos were flightless birds. They lived on Mauritius, an island where they had no **predators** – until humans came in 1505. By the 1680s, people had eaten all the dodos. None have been seen since.

Eggs

Birds lay eggs. So do frogs and toads – and **reptiles**, like snakes and turtles. But **mammals** bear live young, don't they?

This is almost completely true – but not quite! There are actually two kinds of mammal which lay eggs – both from Australia.

One kind is the echidna (say *i-kidna*) or 'spiny anteater'.

The other, the duck-billed platypus, must be one of the strangest animals.

Duck-billed platypuses look so peculiar that when explorers sent a dead one back to England in the 1700s, people thought it was a **hoax**. Had someone attached a duck's bill to a beaver's skin? But no, it is a real animal, and it doesn't just look odd – it spends most of its time in the water, has a poisonous claw and lays eggs, too.

Only birds' eggs have shells. Most other creatures' eggs have leathery outsides.

Stone from water

Water does not always make things wet!

Look at these columns. Can you believe that they were made out of water? Well, it's true…

Some water is 'hard' – it is full of minerals. As hard water drips through a cave, each drop leaves behind a tiny bit of **calcite** (say *cal-sight*). The calcite slowly builds up to make a stone column on the ceiling or floor of the cave.

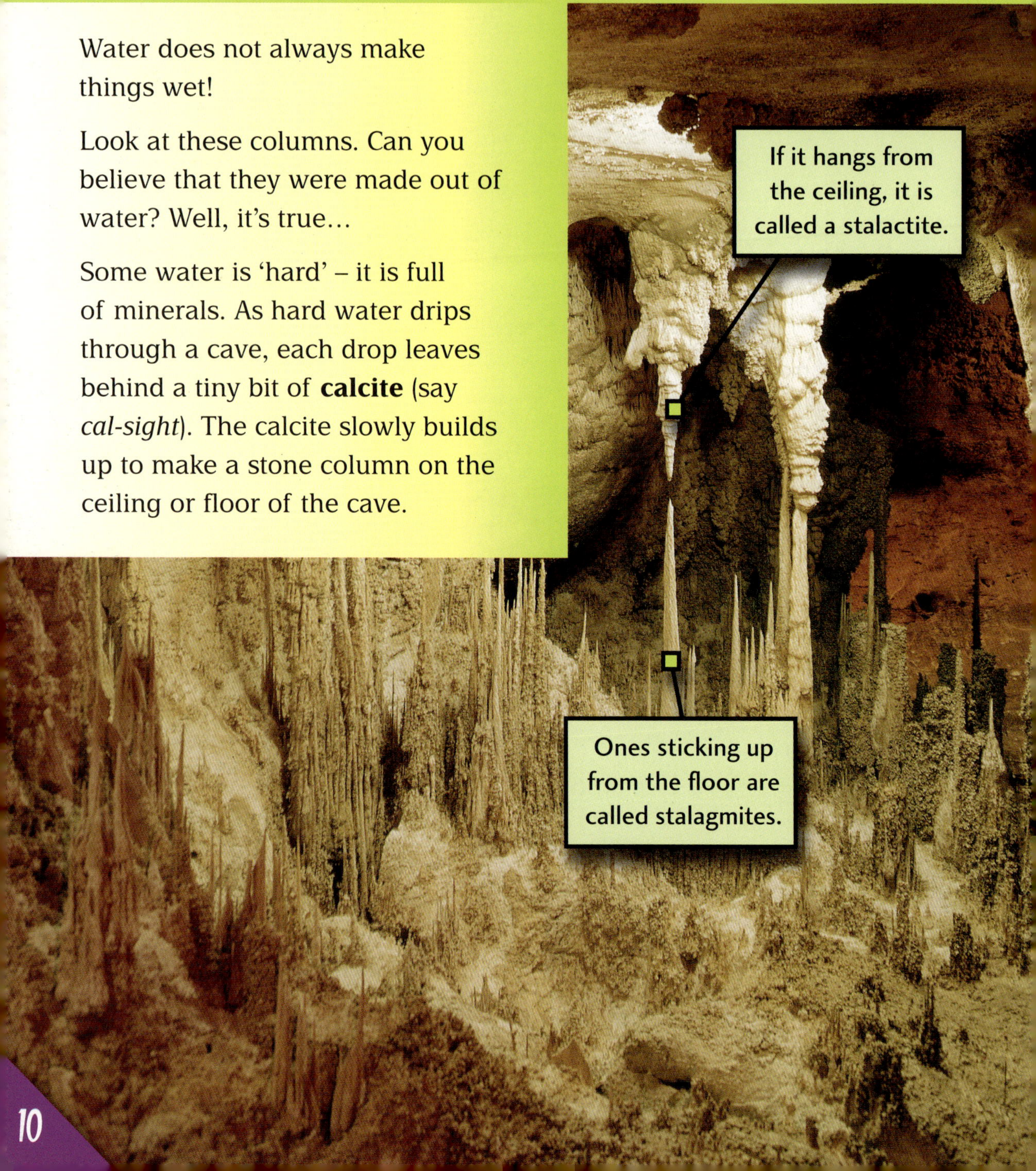

At Mother Shipton's Cave in North Yorkshire, there is a '**petrifying well**': the hard water builds up a covering of stone over everything it wets. People hang things in the water, to see how it works.

Things that soak up water easily, like this teddy bear, take 3–5 months to turn to stone.

Males and females

We all know that men don't have babies; nor do other male animals. It is only the females that give birth – except for seahorses ...

Seahorses are the only animal where the male bears the young. The female puts her eggs into a pouch in the male's belly. Once he has **fertilised** them, he holds the growing young inside his body until he gives birth.

The male seahorse gives birth by pumping young out into the sea.

Did you know that some animals are both male and female at the same time? They are called hermaphrodites (say *her-maf-rodites*). Most hermaphrodites are little water creatures – kinds of snails and worms.

Another hermaphrodite is the sponge. As sponges have both male and female parts, they can take either role when it comes to making new sponges. However, did you even know that sponges are animals? They don't look like animals at all – and they spend their whole adult life fixed to a rock!

Set in stone

Sculpture is generally made to last. It is made out of things like stone or metal, which keep their shape for a very long time.

Some of the oldest things made by people are little statues like this.

Other statues and sculptures, like this one, are set up to remind people of important things that happened, or of famous people.

Sir Winston Churchill was a very important leader of the United Kingdom.

This fountain is a sculpture to remind people of Princess Diana.

But did you know that some artists make sculptures that are meant to fall apart, or to last only a short time? This sculpture was made by carving a block of snow. Snow sculptures often melt as soon as they are finished.

There is more information on the next two pages about sculptures which are made *not* to last.

Art in the making

Some artists work mainly on things that will not last very long. For them, art is about making the work, not the work lasting forever.

Weymouth is famous for its sand sculptures. Fred Darrington made them for over 70 years, and now his grandson Mark Anderson carries on the tradition. The sculptures last a lot longer than sandcastles, unless a very high tide sweeps them away.

One of Mark Anderson's sand sculptures.

On beaches across the world, there are competitions to make sand sculptures. Whole families can get involved, all over the beach.

The American artist Patrick Dougherty makes work out of sticks. He weaves them together into large structures, 'using sticks as a drawing material', he says. His open-air sculptures gradually fall apart and return to nature.

These sculptures are part of a display called 'Call of the Wild'.

Building blocks

What do you think of when you imagine a building? Probably something roughly square, like a house or an office block.

Most modern houses are more or less boxes – the walls are flat and fit together at corners. Their shape makes it easy to fit a lot into a small space like the houses below.

But not all buildings are square – think about lighthouses. It must be interesting to make furniture that will fit their round rooms!

Old castles often have round parts, like towers or turrets. Some **prehistoric** castles, like the Scottish brochs, are completely round.

This broch on one of the Shetland Islands is over 2000 years old.

Modern public buildings can be odd shapes, like 30 St Mary Axe in London – people call it 'The Gherkin' because of its unusual shape.

The next two pages are about an **architect** who made buildings that weren't square or round – just sort of wiggly.

Gaudí

The Spanish architect, Antoni Gaudí (say *gow-dee*), didn't seem to like straight lines – so his buildings look really strange.

This house in Barcelona, called Casa Mila, was finished in 1911. It is wiggly and knobbly and looks so little like a building that the locals call it 'la Pedrera' – the **quarry**. There are no straight lines in the building, and no **right angles**, either inside or out.

From above, the Gaudí staircase looks like a snail shell.

Gaudí said his ideas came from 'the great book of nature' and his buildings do seem to have 'grown' rather than been built.

Gaudí's greatest project was this cathedral, Sagrada Familia (the Holy Family). He worked on it for over 25 years, but only finished this one end.

Work is still going on to complete Sagrada Familia. Although it is still unfinished, it is the most visited attraction in Barcelona.

Up and down

What happens when you throw something up? It comes down! It can fall fast, like a ball, or float slowly down, like a parachute. The Earth pulls everything towards it, with an invisible force called gravity.

But have you ever dropped a helium balloon? It floats up, because the gas inside it is lighter than air. However, gravity catches up with helium balloons, too, in the end.

The only way to escape from gravity is to use a rocket and a huge amount of fuel. You have to travel at about 8000 kilometres per hour to get into space.

It's exciting to know we can travel into space. It's also nice to know that however high you jump, you will always come back down to Earth.

In the same way, it's nice to know that most things follow the rules. But isn't the world far more interesting because it doesn't always work the way we expect it to?

Glossary

architect – someone who designs buildings

calcite – a kind of stone made of crystals

fertilised – to join a male animal's 'seeds' to a female's eggs to produce young

hoax – something made up to fool people

mammals – animals that, as babies, feed on their mother's milk

petrifying well – a well that turns things to stone

predators – animals which eat other animals

prehistoric – the time before any history was written down

quarry – a place where stone is cut out of the ground

reptiles – animals with scaly skin and cold blood

right angle – the kind of corner you see in a square

Index